101 Games to Play

Compiled by Elizabeth Cooper

TREASURE PRESS

First published in Great Britain in 1981 by
The Hamlyn Publishing Group Limited

This edition published in 1989 by
Treasure Press
Michelin House
81 Fulham Road
London SW3 6RB

Reprinted 1990

© Copyright The Hamlyn Publishing Group Limited 1981

ISBN 1 85051 394 5

Printed in Portugal

Contents

8

Introduction

For many of these games, you will need a grown-up's help. Ask permission if you are going to play a noisy indoor game. Remember, you might wake someone up!

When you need things to help you play a game, there is a list given – ask a grown-up to help you find them. All the things are everyday objects which can be found around the house.

For party games, it is a good idea to have a prize for the winner – a sweet or a balloon is a pleasant suprise.

All the games in the section on card games can also be played at parties. If there are lots of children, take it in turns to play the games. Those who are not in a game can watch and cheer on the players, or perhaps play a different game outside. There are more card games included in other sections, such as 'Games for One or Two'.

In the game 'Redlight, Greenlight' on page 28, you can find out how to choose someone to be IT using the rhyme *Eeny, meeny, miney, moe.*

Number Puzzles

Here are some clever number puzzles to try out on a friend.
For the first one, tell your friend to do the following:
Think of a number. Double it. Add ten. Divide by two. Now
take away the number you first thought of. The answer is
five.

   The second puzzle is a little different:
Think of a number. Add seven. Multiply by two. Take away
four. Take away the number you first thought of. Add one.
Ask your friend what number he ended up with. Take eleven
off the number he tells you. This will give you the number
that he started with. He will be very surprised when you tell
him what the number was.

Knucklebones

You will need:
five small pebbles

This game was played by the ancient Greeks hundreds of years ago. Another name for it is Five Stones. The Greeks played it with five matching bones, but you can use small pebbles instead. They should be the same size.

You can do lots of things with them. First put them in the palm of your hand and toss them up in the air. Spread your fingers and catch as many as you can on the back of your hand.

Now try something different. Put four of the pebbles down and keep one in your hand. Throw this one up in the air. Before you catch it, pick up one of the four pebbles with the same hand. Try picking up two of the pebbles next, then three, then four.

Take turns at these tricks with your friend. The more you practise, the easier they will become.

Double Writing

You will need:
coloured pencils
paper

Have your box of coloured pencils and some paper handy for this trick. It is fun to try when you are sitting quietly on your own or with a friend.

Fasten two coloured pencils together with a rubber band or by tying some string round them. Move one of them down so that the points are not quite level.

Hold the pencils with the longer one on top, so that the points touch the paper at the same time. Now you are ready to do some double writing. You could write your name to start with, then a sentence. See how the colours look, then go on and try some others.

Finger Shadow Game

You will need:
a light or torch

To play this game all you use are your hands, a bright light and a clear wall. Hold up your hands with the light shining behind them and make the shapes of a bird flying, a dog and a sheep. The picture shows you how to do it. Try and make some shapes of your own.

Roll Call

You will need:
a pack of cards

Roll Call is an easy card game for beginners. It is a game of patience and is for playing on your own.

Find a pack of cards and shuffle them. Now turn them face upwards one at a time. As you turn them, say 'Ace, two, three,' and so on up to King. Then start all over again with 'Ace'. When you turn over a card that is the same as the number you are saying, take it out of the pack and put it aside.

Keep going through the pack and counting. You win the game if you are able to put all the cards aside.

Puss in the Corner

You will need:
a pack of cards

This is a different sort of patience game for one player. It is called a building-up patience, and you will see why.

First look through the pack of cards and take out the four Aces. Lay them out on the table or floor to make a square. Think of the Aces as the foundations of a house. All the other cards are the bricks. The idea of the game is to build up the bricks on top of the foundations – red goes on red and black goes on black. You must build up the cards in this order: Ace, two, three, four, five, six, seven, eight, nine, ten, Jack, Queen, King.

Deal four cards from the rest of the pack and lay them one at a time at the four corners of the square. These are called the

18

waste heaps. Now look at the four cards and see if you can build on to the Aces with them. Our picture shows an example. The two of Clubs can be put on top of either the Ace of Spades or the Ace of Clubs.

To build on the foundations you can use only the top cards from the waste heaps. If you turn up a seven you may move one waste heap on to another, and then split one of the two remaining heaps so that you still have four.

When you are playing a card on a waste heap you should try and place it on a high card rather than a low one. If you cannot do this you should play it on a heap that does not contain another card of the same rank (number).

If the game does not come out in the first deal, you are allowed to have another. Pick up the four waste heaps and put them together without shuffling them. Then begin the second deal.

Sevenses

You will need:
a ball

Sevenses is fun to play on your own or with a friend. It is called Sevenses because there are seven parts to it. Take a small rubber ball or tennis ball outdoors with you, and find a wall to throw it against.

Start with the number seven – throw the ball against the wall seven times and catch it as it falls. You can use both hands.

Now for number six – throw the ball against the wall and let it bounce on the ground before you catch it. Do this six times.

You do not need the wall for number five – with the flat of your hand, bounce the ball on the ground five times without stopping. Catch it at the end.

Number four is harder – lift one leg off the ground and throw the ball at the wall under your knee. Catch it as it

bounces back, before it falls. Do this four times.

Number three is harder still – throw the ball against the wall and when it comes back, bounce it on the ground twice with your hand, then hit it back to the wall. Catch it before it bounces. Do this three times.

Number two – throw the ball at the wall and let it bounce back to you. You have to turn right around before you catch it. Do this twice.

And finally, number one – throw the ball against the wall and quickly clap your hands behind your back before you catch it. Do not let it bounce. Do this once.

The aim of the game is to go through all the numbers without making a mistake. If you do make a mistake pass the ball to your friend. When it is your turn again, you can either start where you left off or, to make it harder, go back to the beginning.

Go through the game using both hands first. Then try catching the ball one-handed. To make the game really difficult, play it with a blindfold over your eyes.

Marble Bowls

You will need:
a small cardboard box
some marbles

Here is a different way of using marbles – in a game of bowls.
You can play on your own or with a friend.

Make a scoring box out of a cardboard box. All you have
to do is cut some arches in one side of it. It should also be
open at the bottom. Above the arches write a score number.
Now stand back and roll the marbles through the arches.
Then count your score.

Conkers

You will need:
some horse chestnuts
string

Conkers used to be made from snails' shells! Now the game is played with big brown horse chestnuts.

Go out with a friend and find some horse chestnuts. Ask your mother or father to make a hole through the chestnuts with a skewer and to bake them in an oven at low heat to make them hard. Cut two pieces of string 30 centimetres long and tie a knot at one end of each. Thread a string through each conker.

Now you are ready to play the game. Hold out your conker on its string. Your friend now winds her string round the fingers of her right hand. She leaves about 10 centimetres of it free to pull back against her thumb. She then holds the conker in her left hand and pulls the string against the thumb of her right hand. She lets it go with a jerk. If she is lucky it will hit your conker and shatter it. Her conker is then called a 'oner'. If she scores a second time with a new opponent, it is called a 'twoer' and so on. If she misses, it is your turn.

If one of you shatters a 'twoer' you add two on to your score, and another one for breaking the conker. The aim is to get as high a score as possible.

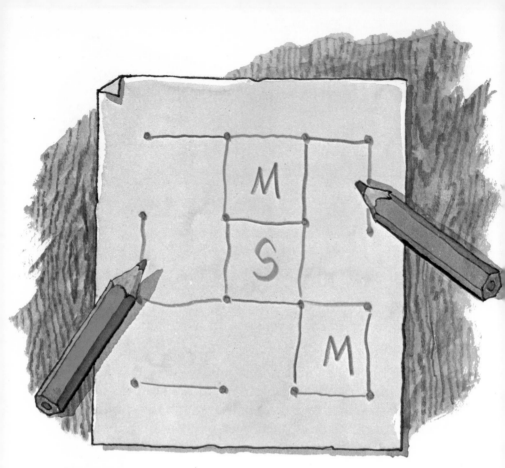

Dots

You will need:
two coloured pencils
paper

Dots is another simple game for two players. To play it, use two differently coloured pencils and a piece of paper. Make lines of dots on the paper. You can have as many as you like.

The first player draws a line between any two dots. The second player does the same. Play continues like this until one player draws in the fourth side of a square. That square now belongs to her and she can put her initial in it.

The winner is the person who completes the most squares.

Hangman

You will need:
a pencil
paper

Hangman is a word game. Two can play.

One player – we shall call him David – thinks of a word. He shows the other player, Jenny, how many letters the word has by marking dashes on the paper. He also draws in a line for the base of the gallows.

Jenny must now try and guess at the letters in the word. If she gets one right, David writes it in wherever it comes in the word. As soon as Jenny suggests a letter that is not in the word, David draws in the first line of the gallows. Jenny has to try and guess the whole word before she is hung. When all the lines have been drawn in, the gallows should look like the ones in the picture.

Running and Jumping Games

Simon Says

Choose one player to stand out in front of the group. He tells you what to do. You must obey him whenever he says something that starts with 'Simon says'. If he calls 'Simon says pat your head', you pat your head. If he calls 'Simon says circle your arms like a windmill', you circle your arms like a windmill. But if he gives you an order without the 'Simon says' you must stand quite still. If you move the tiniest bit you are out. The one to stay in the longest is the winner. She becomes the next Simon.

Redlight, Greenlight

There should be at least three of you to play this. First choose someone to be IT by saying this rhyme:

Eeny, meeny, miney, moe
Catch a tiger by the toe
If he hollers let him go
Eeny, meeny, miney, MOE!

Point to the players in turn as you say each word. Whoever you end with is IT.

Now you are ready to begin. Stand in a line about 9 metres away from the player who is IT. The IT turns her back to you and calls out, 'Greenlight, one, two, three, four, five, six, seven, eight, nine, ten, redlight!' As soon as you hear 'greenlight', start running towards the IT. When you hear 'redlight' you must stop running because the IT will turn around. If she catches one of you moving after she says 'redlight' that player must go back to the starting line.

The player who is the first to tap the IT on the shoulder is the winner. He becomes the next IT.

What's the Time, Mr Wolf?

The more players you have for this game, the more fun it is.
Choose a Mr Wolf by saying *Eeny, meeny, miney, moe.*

Mr Wolf walks away and the rest of you follow him. Now
you all say loudly 'What's the time, Mr Wolf?' Mr Wolf
answers with the time. He can say any time he likes. When he
answers 'Twelve o'clock, dinner time,' you must all run as
fast as you can back to the start. Mr Wolf runs after you. The
person he catches or the last one home is the next Mr Wolf.

Giant Dice Game

You will need:
an empty tea packet
glue or sticky tape
plain paper
a pencil

Ask a grown-up to help you make a really big dice from an empty tea packet. This is how you do it. Cut off one end and cut down along the corners. Fold the four sides down to close the end, and you have a cube. Cover it by sticking on plain paper. Draw on the dots from one to six. Make them really clear.

Now you are ready to play a game with your dice. Here is a good one for several children. Stand on one side of a large room or outside in the garden. Make a starting line and a finish.

Throw the dice and take a big step for each dot that comes up. Take it in turns. The first person to reach the finish is the winner.

31

Foxes and Hounds

Find a big open space for this game if you can. Divide into two groups. Try and make equal numbers. One group are the foxes and the other group are the hounds.

The foxes run off as fast as they can while the hounds count to ten. The hounds then set out after them.

As soon as a fox is touched by one of the hounds, he becomes a hound and helps hunt down the other foxes.

The hunt goes on until all the foxes have been caught. Divide into different groups the second time round, so that you take turns at being foxes and hounds.

Cherry Drop

You will need:
a blindfold (a scarf or a piece of cloth)

Play Cherry Drop with three or more players. Choose one of them to be the cherry tree. Put a blindfold on him. He then stands with his arms and fingers outspread like the branches of the tree. The other players are the cherries on the tree. They each hold on to one finger of the blindfolded player.

The cherry tree asks 'Are you ready?' When the cherries answer 'Yes', the cherry tree counts to ten as fast as he can while the cherries run from the tree. When the cherry tree gets to ten he yells 'Cherry drop!' and all the cherries stop running and stand still. The cherry tree, wearing his blindfold, then goes looking for all the cherries. The last player to be found is the winner. He becomes the next tree.

Minefield

You will need:
two blindfolds (scarves or pieces of cloth)
cardboard boxes

You will have to be very careful where you tread in this game. Play it with a big group of friends and divide them into two teams. It does not matter where you play it, but a large room or hall is a good place. You could also play it outside.

Fill the playing area with large things such as boxes and chairs. These are the mines and the playing area is the minefield.

Now blindfold one person from each team. They have to cross the minefield without touching any mines. The other members of their team can help by calling out to them where they should go next. If either of them touches a mine, they have to stop while their team counts aloud to ten. When they finally reach the end of the minefield, they take off the blindfolds and run back to the start. The next players put on the blindfolds and go through the minefield.

The winning team is the one to get all its members through first. They must all sit down at the end.

Hopscotch

You will need:
a stone
a piece of chalk

Find a nice clear stretch of concrete or asphalt near your house or at school. With a piece of white chalk draw a rectangle about 2·5 metres long and 2 metres wide. Divide it into twelve squares and give each square a number. You can have up to four players.

The first player throws a small flat stone so that it lands in one of the squares.

If the stone lands outside the rectangle or on a line, she loses her turn and the next player goes.

If the stone lands in a square, the thrower hops through the other squares until she gets to her stone. She then writes her initials in that square, and hops back to the start. If she touches a line on the way, she loses the turn and has to rub out her initials.

If a player lands in any square with any initials, it is called a foul and his turn stops straight away. The best idea is to get your stone into the furthest square first. Otherwise you will have to hop over the nearest squares with your initials.

The winner is the player who wins the most squares.

Shipwreck

The smaller you are the better, for this game. It should be played with a lot of children out of doors or in a large room. There should be some old furniture or other large objects such as boxes dotted around.

One person is the leader. He calls out 'Shipwreck' and names a piece of furniture or other objects. For example, he could say 'Shipwreck – table' or 'Shipwreck – wooden steps'. All the other players try and climb on to the object. Those who cannot squeeze on, or who fall off, are out of the game. As more and more players are out, the leader names smaller and smaller things to climb on to.

Sticky Toffee

This is a tag game. In the simplest sort of tag game, one person chases the others until she touches someone. That person then becomes IT. Sticky Toffee is more complicated. You play it like this.

Choose someone to be IT. Everybody runs off and the IT chases them. As soon as she touches one of them, that player has to join hands with the IT. They now both try to catch the other players. Whoever is touched by one of the ITs must join on to the line. You will soon have a long chain of ITs. The last player to be caught becomes the new IT.

Snail Hop

You will need:
a piece of chalk

This is a hopping game a bit like hopscotch, but you draw a coiled or snail shape to hop in, rather than a rectangle. This is how you play it.

Draw a snail shape on the ground with chalk. Mark it off in sections. Make them all different sizes. The game can be as hard as you want to make it, but each section must be big enough to fit one foot inside without touching the lines.

Now you can start. Take it in turns to hop on one foot from the start right round the coil to the centre of the 'snail'. You must hop in each section, and you are not allowed to touch any lines. If you do, you must go back and wait for your next turn. When you get to the centre you are allowed to rest on both feet. Then you must hop back to the start. You can use the other foot on the way back if you want to.

When you have hopped to the centre and back again, you may write your initials in one of the sections. It does not matter which one you write them in. This becomes your section and you are allowed to rest both feet in it for the rest of the game. All the other players have to hop over it.

The game is over when every section has some initials in it. The winner is the player with the most initialled sections.

Character Freeze

This game will be a favourite with anyone who likes acting.
It is best to have a lot of people playing it because there are
more funny faces to look at.

Use a big playing area. Stand some distance apart. Choose
someone to be leader. She calls 'Freeze' and everyone stands
still. Then she says 'When I say unfreeze, everyone will
be . . . ' and names a character from a story or a film, or from
everyday life. It could be Father Christmas, Dracula, a wicked
witch, Prince Charming, Superman, or your teacher. When
the leader says 'Unfreeze!' everybody must pretend to be the
character named. You can move about wherever you like. It
might be fun to take a few photographs of people.

Stuck in the Mud

Stuck in the Mud is another tag game. Whenever a person is tagged he has to stand in one spot with his legs apart and his arms outstretched and shout for help. A player who has not yet been tagged can crawl between his legs to set him free again.

If you only have one IT, it is very easy to be set free. Choose two or three ITs so that it is easier to catch more people.

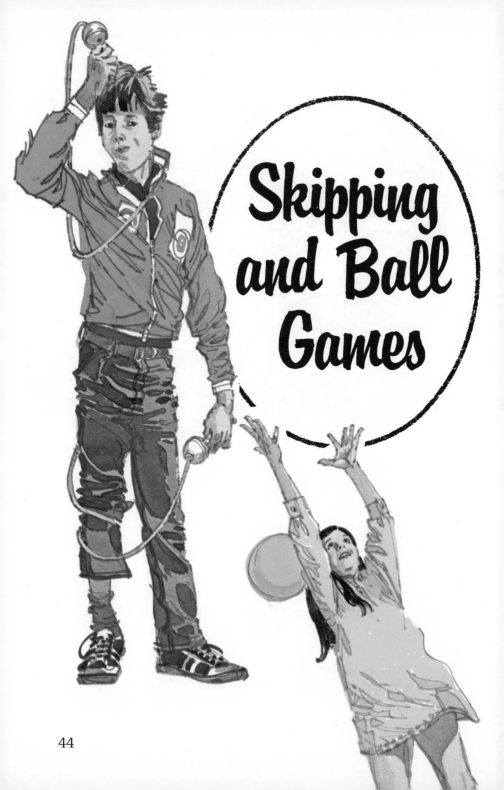

Skipping and Ball Games

Circle Ball

You will need:
a ball
a long string
a piece of cloth or net

Play this with a number of people. Find a large ball and tie it to a long string. The best way to do this is to wrap the ball in cloth or a piece of net, and tie the string to that.

Players stand in a large circle. One person stands in the middle of the circle and swings the ball around on the end of the string. The players have to jump over the ball as it swings around.

As soon as a player is touched by the ball, she is out. The last one to be out is the winner.

Rounders

You will need:
a bat or stick
a ball

Have two teams for this ball game. Six in each team is enough, but you can have any number up to ten. Play it on grass if you can.

First mark out your field. You want a batting area and four bases arranged in a circle and with about 10 metres from one base to the next. One team fields and the other bats.

There should be one fielder standing at each base and some further out in case the ball is hit a long way. One of the fielders is the bowler and another is the 'backstop'. He stands behind the batsman.

The bowler stands in the middle of the circle and throws the ball underarm to the first batsman. If the batsman hits it, she must run to first base, and still further if she has time. She must touch each base on her way round. If she gets all the way round before the ball is returned to the bowler, she scores a rounder. If not, she waits at a base until the next person hits the ball. The batsman has to run outside the circle.

There are several ways of getting a player out. While players run between the bases a fielder can touch the next base with the ball. The bowler can also bounce the ball in the batting area while the batsman is between bases. The batsman is also out if the ball that she hits is caught by one of the fielders before it bounces.

When there is no one left to bat, the teams change over and the fielders go in to bat.

The team with the most rounders wins.

Broken Bottles

You will need:
a ball

This is a good warming-up game for rounders because it gives you practice in catching and throwing the ball.

Find a few friends – six would be about the right number. They should stand in a circle with one player in the middle. He throws the ball to each of the others in turn. They must try and catch it. If a player drops the ball he must pay for his mistake the next time round – he must catch the ball with one hand only. If he drops it again, he must catch it with the other hand when it is next thrown to him. The next penalty is to catch it while he is on one knee, then two knees and finally sitting down. If the player does not catch it sitting down, he is out. If the player catches it again before he is out, he can go back through all the positions in the next rounds until he is standing again.

Piggy in the Middle

You will need:
a ball

This is a simple game for three. Two people stand a few metres apart facing each other. The piggy stands in the middle. He has to try and catch the ball as it is thrown between the other two players. If the ball is dropped, any of the players can run for it.

As soon as the piggy catches the ball, he goes to the outside. The person who threw the ball is the new piggy.

French Cricket

You will need:
a cricket bat or flat piece of wood
a soft ball

The best place to play French Cricket is on the beach, but a garden or park will do just as well. If you do not have a cricket bat you can use a heavy flat piece of wood or a tennis racket. You will also need a soft ball. Two players will enjoy this game, but it is much more fun with a lot of people.

What you must try and do is stop the bowler from hitting your legs below the knees with the ball. You may hold the bat anywhere in front of your legs. You are out if the ball hits your legs or if you hit the ball and it is then caught by one of the other players. The only time you may turn round to score a run is when none of the players are holding the ball.

To score a run you pass the bat round your body, changing it from hand to hand behind your back. Each time you pass it round counts as one run.

Wibble Wobble Jelly

You will need:
a rope

Here is a rhyme to skip to with your friends. One person skips while two others turn the rope. This is how the rhyme goes:

Jelly on a plate,
Jelly on a plate,
Wibble, wobble, wibble, wobble,
Jelly on a plate.

Sausages in the pan,
Sausages in the pan,
Turn them over, turn them over,
Sausages in the pan.

Ghostie in the house,
Ghostie in the house,
Turn him out, turn him out,
Ghostie in the house.

The actions are easy to remember. When they come to 'Wibble, wobble, wibble, wobble', the rope-turners wobble the rope from side to side. As everyone chants 'Turn them over, turn them over', they turn the rope quickly. The skipper has to jump very fast. At 'Turn him out, turn him out', he has to run out of the rope.

Baby in the Cradle

You will need:
a rope

Two players turn the skipping rope and say this rhyme while
a third skips in time:
Baby in the cradle, fast asleep,
How many hours does she sleep?

The rope is then turned very fast, and the skipper tries
hard to keep up. The number of hours the baby sleeps are the
number of skips the player can do.

Birthdays

You will need:
a long rope

This is another skipping game for a group. If you use a long rope with one person at each end, several of you will be able to skip at the same time.

It is very easy to play. As you all skip you call out the months of the year – January, February, March and so on. As soon as you hear your birthday month called you run out and another player takes your place.

Team
Games

Bean Toss

You will need:
dried beans
three bowls
a pencil
paper

If you have a large number of players, divide them into two teams. All you use to play the game are a handful of dried beans, three bowls fitting loosely one inside another and a pencil and paper to keep the score.

Put the 'nest' of bowls at one end of a table. Players now stand at the other end and take it in turns to toss beans into the bowls. The smallest bowl counts three points, the middle size bowl counts two points, and the biggest counts one point. You are not allowed to touch the table.

After each player's throw, count the beans in the different bowls and work out his points. Keep count for each team. The team with the highest score wins.

Fill the Bucket

You will need (for each team):
two buckets
one saucer

Have about five or six people in each team. There will be water spilling everywhere so play the game outside on the grass. It is lots of fun.

For each team find two buckets and a saucer. One bucket

should be filled with water, and the other left empty. Place the empty one about 20 metres away from the full one.

The first member of the team fills the saucer with water from the full bucket, runs to the empty bucket and pours the water in. He then turns back to the start and passes the saucer to the next person who does the same thing.

The winning team is the first to transfer all the water into the empty bucket – you will have to be very careful not to spill any.

Long Jump

You will need an even number of players for this jumping game. Any number between ten and twenty will do. Divide into two equal teams and choose a leader for each. Line up behind them at the start.

Each leader makes a standing jump from the start. The next team member jumps from where the leader landed, and so on down the line until the last player has her turn.

Now measure the distances jumped. The team which jumps the furthest wins.

Under and Over Ball

You will need:
a ball

Make up two teams of about six players each. Line up behind each other with spaces between you. Stand with legs apart.

The first person in each team bends down and tosses the ball backwards between his legs to the next player. She catches it and tosses it over her head to the player behind her. He in his turn tosses it under and the next team member tosses it over until it reaches the last player. He catches the ball and runs with it to the front of the line.

Repeat until the first person in each team has worked his way back to the front of the line. The first team to finish are the winners.

Potato Race

You will need:
some potatoes
spoons
handkerchiefs
a bucket

Ask a grown-up if you can have about twelve potatoes from the kitchen for this game. Get several spoons, some large handkerchiefs for blindfolds and a bucket.

Divide into two teams of two or more. Put the potatoes in a line about 15 metres away and place the bucket nearby.

Blindfolds are put on the members of one team, and they are given their spoons. They now have two minutes to make their way to the potatoes and spoon them into the bucket. The other team watches. It is a very funny sight.

After two minutes the potatoes are counted. They are then laid out on the ground again. Now it is the other team's turn to spoon potatoes into the bucket.

The team with the most potatoes in the bucket wins.

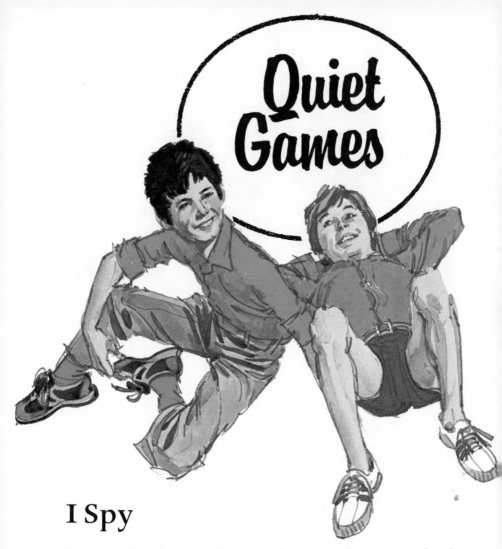

Quiet Games

I Spy

You can play this anywhere – at home, in the car, at school, even while you are out walking.

It is a very simple game. One person says 'I spy with my little eye something that starts with . . . ' and gives the first letter of an object in sight (such as P for PENCIL). The other players have to look around them and guess what the object might be.

The person who gets it right is the next one to spy something.

Sleeping Tigers

This is one of the quietest games you can play. You will need a group of friends.

Pretend that you are tigers in a deep, dark jungle. You are very sleepy. One person sits out in front and counts to ten. He watches while the others lie down and go to sleep. The tigers must try not to move. Anyone who is seen moving must sit out with the person at the front and watch for other twitching tigers.

The last person to be caught out is the King of the Jungle.

Heads and Bodies

You will need:
paper
pencils

If you feel like drawing some funny pictures, try Heads and Bodies. It is a game for two or more. Cut some long, narrow pieces of paper and find some pencils.

Each person has a piece of paper and draws a head and neck on it. It can be the head of a person or of an animal.

Everyone then folds the paper so that only the bottom of the neck can be seen.

Once everyone has finished, they pass their papers to the player on the left of them.

Each player now draws a body to fit on to the neck. The body should finish at the top of the legs. Papers are folded again and passed on.

This time players add legs and the next time, feet. Then the papers are folded and, for the last time, passed on.

Unfold all the papers. Be ready for a big surprise!

Beetle

You will need:
paper
pencils

Here is another dice game. Use the dice made for the game on page 30 or a small plastic one. Find some paper and a pencil for each player.

Take it in turns to throw the dice. The first person to throw a six starts the game. She throws again. Whatever number she throws, she can draw a part of a beetle. This is what the numbers mean:

six – the body
five – the head
four – the two front legs
three – the four back legs
two – the eyes
one – the antennae

The idea of the game is to go on throwing the dice and drawing parts of the beetle until it is complete. The first player to have a finished beetle is the winner.

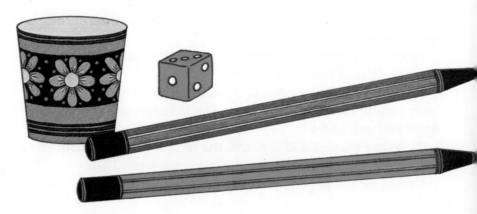

69

School

You will need:
a pebble or coin

Play School on a short flight of stairs. If you do not have any in the house, perhaps you could find some outside in the park or playground, at a friend's house or even at school. Play the game with a few of your friends. Before you start, find a pebble or coin.

One player is the teacher. He stands in front of the steps. The others are his class. They sit on the bottom step facing the teacher. This step is called 'first grade'.

The teacher is in charge of the pebble or coin. He holds his hands behind his back and hides the pebble in one of them. Then he makes fists of his hands and holds them out in front where the 'class' can see them. He asks one of the class to guess which hand has the pebble. If he guesses correctly he moves up one step. This step is called second grade. The teacher asks all the members of his class in turn to guess where the pebble is. Those who get it right move up a step. Those who get it wrong move down one. (If they are on the first step they stay where they are.)

The winner is the first person to reach the top step. He becomes the teacher next time round.

70

Shadows

You will need:
an old sheet
a lamp

Shadows is a game for several players. Divide into two teams.

Ask a grown-up to help you hang an old sheet across the room and put a bright lamp behind it. Turn off the other lights.

To play the game, the members of each team pass between the lamp and the sheet one at a time, and try to disguise themselves with different actions. You can limp, stride, hunch your back, wiggle from side to side or do anything else you like to fool the members of the other team. They are watching from the other side of the sheet and have to guess who the shadows belong to.

Tiddlywinks

You will need:
a plastic bowl
coloured plastic discs

Tiddlywinks is a simple game but lots of fun, especially when played by a group. It is also possible for one person to play on his own.

Ask your mother for a kitchen bowl. You will also need a number of differently coloured plastic discs or small flat buttons. There should be several of each colour. These are the tiddlywinks. Find some larger discs too – one for each player.

Pass the discs out to the players. Each person should have tiddlywinks of one colour. Now sit in a circle and line up the tiddlywinks around the bowl, about 60 centimetres away.

Take it in turns to try and flip your tiddlywinks into the bowl. To do this take your large disc and press on the back edge of a small tiddlywink with it. The tiddlywink should go flying. If you are lucky it will land in the bowl.

The person who gets the most tiddlywinks into the bowl is the winner.

Let's Go Fishing

You will need:
paper
paper clips
magnets
string
sticks

You do not have to go down to the river to play this game. You can go fishing in your very own house.

Cut out some fish from pieces of card. Slip a paper clip on to each one and scatter the shapes on the floor. Now tie a magnet to a string on a stick and see how many fish shapes you can pick up. Play it with your friends. The person who catches the most fish is the winner.

Bottle Music

You will need:
**seven empty bottles
a ruler or stick**

You can play this on your own or with a friend. It is best played in the garden as it is easy to spill water out of the bottles.

Find seven empty bottles. They should all be the same kind. Fill them with water to different levels. Tap the bottles with a piece of wood or a ruler. Each will make a different musical note. Now try and play a simple tune on them.

Up Jenkins

You will need:
a coin

The rest of your family might enjoy playing this with you. You need several people to make two teams.

The teams sit on opposite sides of a table. Each team has a leader. One of the teams has a small coin which it must try and keep hidden from the other team. The members of the team pass it to each other beneath the table.

The leader of the other team gives orders to the team with the coin. When he says 'Up Jenkins' they must put their hands on the table, fists clenched. He may then tell them to:

creepy crawly –this means moving the fingers in a kind of crawl.

flat on table – unclenching hands and laying them flat on the table.

wibbly wobbly – turning clenched fists over and back on the table.

The members of the other team now try and guess who has the coin. If they guess correctly, they take the coin and hide it. If they do not guess, the team with the coin has another turn at passing the coin under the table.

Battleships

You will need:
squared paper
two pencils

This is a game for two players. To play it all you use are
four pieces of squared paper (12 squares by 12 squares) and
one pencil each. Along the edge of the paper, letter the
squares A to L down and one to twelve across.

You have two pieces of squared paper each. Take one of
them and think of it as the ocean. Now, with your pencil,
mark in six ships as follows:

one battleship – five squares in a row

two destroyers – three squares each

two submarines – one square each

one corvette – one square

Your fleet can go anywhere on the ocean. You must keep your
paper hidden from the other player.

To start the game, one player fires a shot at his opponent's
ships. He might say 'I am firing at B5'. This is because he
thinks that this square might have a ship in it. To remember
which square he has fired at, he marks it on his spare piece of
paper. All the squares covered by a ship must be hit, one at a
time, to sink the ship.

His opponent tells him if he has scored a hit on any of her
ships and, if he has, crosses the square off her paper. She
now fires her first shot.

The game continues like this until one player sinks all the
ships of the opponent. This player is then the winner.

Fortunes

You will need:
paper
scissors
a pencil

Instead of telling fortunes with a crystal ball, try using this paper fortune teller. It is quite easy to make and you can use it on all your friends.

Cut a square of paper with sides about 10 centimetres long. Then fold the four corners into the centre and crease.

Turn the paper over. Write fortunes in each corner. They can be just a few words, for example, 'You are lucky' or, 'You will be in trouble at school'. Turn these four corners into the centre and crease. Write numbers from one to eight on the

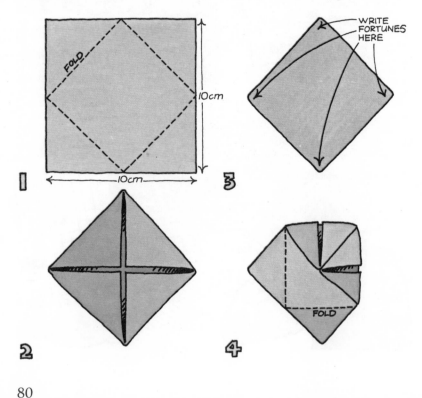

80

eight triangles which the square has now been divided into.

Fold in half across. Open out and fold in half downwards. Turn the square over and fold in half from corner to corner. Open out and fold in half between the other corners. Open out again and then push the four corners together. Put your thumbs and forefingers under the flaps which will now stick out. When you move them you will find that you can open the corners two ways. One way shows four numbers and the other way shows four different numbers.

Now your fortune teller is ready to use. Ask a friend to choose a number between one and four, such as number three. Open and shut the corners three times. Ask your friend to choose one of the numbers showing. Open and shut the corners again. Ask him to choose a third number. Turn back the flap with that number and read your friend's fortune.

Marbles

You will need:
**some marbles
or
very small balls**

There are a number of different marble games. This one is for
two players.

One person rolls a marble along the ground. When it stops,
the second player rolls one of her marbles at it and tries to hit
it. If she does hit it, she takes it and adds it to her collection of
marbles while the first player rolls another marble for her to
try to hit. If not, the first player has another go and tries to
hit the second player's marble. The winner is the person
who takes all the opponent's marbles.

Waistlines

You will need:
some string

This is a good trick to play on your friends. It is a simple guessing game.

Find a piece of string about 1·5 metres long. Arrange it in a circle on the floor. Start pulling on one end of the string to make the circle smaller and ask one of the players to tell you when he thinks the circle is the same size as his waist. Hold the string in that spot and pick it up carefully. Try it around the waist of the person guessing. You will be surprised how small a waist can be!

Going on a Trip

This is a game that you can play anywhere. You could be at home, in the car, on a bus, in a train or in the playground at school. You need two players and you can have more if you like.

The first player says 'I'm going on a trip and I'm going to take . . . ' and names an object. The second player has to repeat this and then add another object. The game continues like this, with each person running through the list of objects and adding a new one. As soon as a player misses out an object or mixes up the order he is out of the game. The winner is the last person to be out. She starts the next game.

Quadruped

Here is another game for a long journey in the car. It is easy to play but you must concentrate for a long time.

The idea of the game is to see who can count the most quadrupeds (four-legged animals) during the journey. The person on the right side of the car counts quadrupeds to the right of the road. The person on the left of the car counts quadrupeds on the left-hand side.

You get one point for each animal. It is bad luck if you pass a school – the player on the school side loses all his points. Before you start the game, you can agree on one animal that is worth ten points. It can be any animal you like, but it should be one that is not likely to be seen often, such as a black pig.

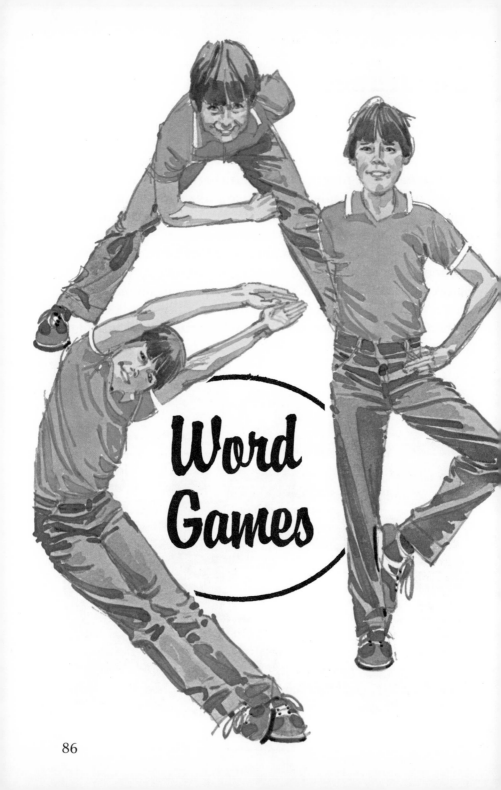

Word
Games

Last Letters

You will need:
pencils
paper

You can have any number of players for this simple game. It is a useful one to play because it helps you with your spelling.

One person calls out the name of something. It could be a town, a river, a country, an animal or a flower. For example, she could call 'daffodil'.

The person on the left of the first player calls out another flower beginning with the last letter of the previous word, for example, 'lilac'. The game continues in this way and anyone who cannot give a word is out. The winner is the last person out.

Long Words

You will need:
pencils
paper

Think of a long word such as *nightingale*. Players have five minutes to write down all the words that they can make out of *nightingale*, such as *night, tin, gale, nail, gate* and so on. They must not be proper names. At the end of the time, count the words you have made and see who has the most.

Animal Word Puzzle

You will need:
pencils
paper

Any number can play this game. One person thinks of the name of an animal. He tells the others how many letters the name has. They have to guess what it is with some help from the name-chooser. This is how it's done.

The players put a dash on their paper for each letter of the word. They number the dashes. The name-chooser then gives them clues to the letters. The first person to guess the word is the winner. She chooses the word in the next round.

Here is an example to show you how the game goes: the word is *hippopotamus*. Players put twelve numbered dashes on their paper like this –

_ _ _ _ _ _ _ _ _ _ _ _

1 2 3 4 5 6 7 8 9 10 11 12

The name-chooser could give the players clues like these –

1. Letters 4, 5 and 6 make a word which means the noise a bubble makes when it bursts (*pop*).

2. Letters 6, 7 and 8 make a word which means a thing that you put a plant in (*pot*).

3. Letters 1, 5 and 6 make a word which means jumping on one foot (*hop*).

The game continues until someone guesses the word. If someone makes the wrong guess, he is out of the game until the next word is chosen.

Hidden Sentence

You will need:
a pencil
paper

How do you hide a sentence? It is easy. All you have to do is add another letter. Look at what is written below. It doesn't look like a sentence, does it? If you look closer you will see that an extra letter has crept in again and again. See if you can find the hidden letter and make out what the sentence says.

YOBUHABVETOBLOOBKVERBYHABRDTOBFIBNDTHIBSBSE-
NBTENCBE

When you have solved this puzzle, try and make up a sentence of your own. Show it to a friend for her to solve.

The sentence says, 'You have to look very hard to find this sentence'. The hidden letter is B.

Make a New Word

You will need:
pencils
paper

Try turning a cake into a lamb. It sounds impossible, but you can do it with words:

1. cake 2. take 3. tame 4. lame 5. lamb

By changing one letter at a time you can gradually make an entirely new word. As you can see, *cake* becomes *take* by changing c to t.

Think of another word that you can change in this way, for example, tame to walk in four stages. Work it out by yourself and then ask a friend to make the new word.

Hiding and Finding Games

Manhunt

You will need four players for this hide and seek game and you can have more if you want to.

Choose one person to hide. She runs off while the rest of the players count to a hundred with their eyes shut. They must not peep.

The person who is hiding can move about as much as she wants to, as long as she remains hidden. The others search for her. As soon as someone spots her, everybody gives chase. The first person to catch her is the next one to run and hide.

Hide and Seek

The best place for a game of hide and seek is outside where there is plenty of space to run around. If you want to play inside, ask a grown-up first, as it can be a very noisy game. This is how you play it.

The first thing to do is choose a place for 'home'. It could be a tree or a garden shed for example. One player is IT. He stands facing 'home' and hides his eyes. When he calls 'On your marks, get set, go!' all the other players run and hide. While they are hiding the IT counts loudly to fifty or a hundred, or sings a song. When he has finished he calls 'Coming, ready or not'. All the players must stop where they are.

The IT then starts looking for the others. As soon as he sees one of the players (for example, Susie who is hiding behind

the hedge) he runs back to home, touches it and calls out 'Tap tap on Susie behind the hedge.' The IT *must* touch home. He must also say who the player is and where she is hiding. If he is right, Susie must come home and be IT in the next game. But if Susie knows that she has been seen she can try and run for home. If she beats the IT home she can call 'Home free.' This means that she is safe and does not have to be IT in the next game.

Whoever is the last home can free the other players. To do this he has to get home before being 'tapped' by the IT. He also has to call 'Home free all!' If he succeeds, the IT player has to be IT again in the next game.

If there are some players that the IT cannot find, and the game is going on for a long time, the IT is allowed to end the game. To do this he calls 'Ally, ally, all in free,' and the players come home then.

Treasure Hunt

You will need:
a pencil
paper
some envelopes

Ask a grown-up to be the organizer of this game. You should have six or more players. Divide them into three teams which should be numbered one, two and three.

The organizer works out ten different hiding places for clues. He writes a clue for each one. For example, if the hiding place is under a wheelbarrow, he could write 'The

next hiding place is under something for wheeling round the garden.' There should be a copy of each clue for every team. The last clue should lead the teams to the treasure which the organizer hides before the start of the game.

The organizer puts each clue in a different envelope marked with the number for each team and leaves the clues in the hiding places. The first clues should be handed out to the teams. The organizer should try and place clues so that the teams go round picking up theirs in a different order. Otherwise it would be easy for them to follow each other around.

The winning team is the one to find the treasure first.

Hares and Hounds

You will need:
some chalk

It is best to play this in the park, on the common or in the countryside where you have plenty of room to run and lay trails. It would be a good game to play on a picnic with a big group of friends.

Choose two people to be the hares. They run off and lay a trail with sticks and stones and arrows drawn in the dirt. They could also take some chalk with them to draw arrows.

They are allowed to lay false trails but they must always lead to a cross so that the hounds will know not to try and go further. Any change in direction must also be clearly marked.

The hares can have fifteen minutes start. All the other players, who are called the hounds, then set out after the hares and try to catch them before they return. If they succeed they are the winners. If the hares reach home without being caught, they have won the game.

Scavenger Hunt

You will need:
paper
pencils
paper bags

The playground would be a good place for this game. You could also play it in the park. Any number can play.

One person makes a list of twenty things for the children to collect – for example, a conker, a bus ticket, a yellow leaf, and so on.

Each player should be given a list and a paper bag for collecting the objects. They have twenty to thirty minutes to complete their Scavenger Hunt. If there are a lot of children they work in pairs.

As the players come back, check through the contents of their bags. The winner of the hunt is the first person to return with all twenty objects.

Games for a Party

Pass the Parcel

You will need:
something to use as a prize
wrapping paper or newspaper
a radio or record player

Find something small that will make a good prize for
someone at your party. It could be a book, a toy, a brightly
coloured comb or something to eat.

Wrap it up in layers and layers of paper and string until it
looks really big.

When it is time to play the game, ask all the children to sit
on the floor in a circle. A grown-up can help you get

everyone organized. They should also work the record player or radio so that you will have some music for the game.

As the music plays, the children pass the parcel around the circle. When the music stops, the person who is holding the parcel keeps it and begins to unwrap it as fast as she can. The game goes on like this with the music stopping and starting until the parcel is finally unwrapped. The person who takes off the final wrapper is the winner and keeps the prize inside.

Artist

You will need:
a felt-tipped pen
a sheet of paper
a blindfold (a scarf or piece of cloth).

This is a very funny game. With help from a grown-up, pin a big sheet of blank paper on the wall.

One person is chosen to be the artist. Put the blindfold on him and give him the pen. Then ask him to draw the main shape of a house or other object. The other children now take it in turns to ask him to add things to the picture, such as a door, windows, a chimney, a garden and people. Unless the artist is extremely clever, his drawing will probably look very messy and funny, and nothing like a house!

Memory Game

You will need:
a tray
pencils
paper
objects from around the house

Most party games are noisy when there are a lot of children. If you feel like something quieter, try the Memory Game. All your guests will be as quiet as mice while they are playing it.

Before the party lay out twelve or more objects on a tray.

You could choose such things as a hairbrush, a button, a candle, an apple, a milk jug and so on.

When you are ready to play the game, carry the tray in to your guests. Tell them to look at it closely for one minute and to memorize all the objects. Take the tray away and hand out some paper and a pencil to each player and ask them all to write down as many objects as they can remember. They can have a few minutes to do this.

They can then swap papers with each other and tick the correct answers as you give them. The winner is the person with the most correct objects.

Musical Bumps

You will need:
a radio

Find a clear space for this game. A big playroom would be perfect. You will need some music, so ask a grown-up to take charge of the radio for you.

While the music is playing, everyone dances around the room. As soon as the music stops the children must fall to the floor. The last one to fall down is out.

The game continues like this until there is only one player left in. He or she is the winner.

Corks

You will need:
some large corks

Imagine trying to say something with a cork in your mouth.
Play this game at your next party and see if you can do it. It is
very simple. Divide the children into three teams. They
should then sit down on the floor facing each other.

One team decides on a general knowledge question to ask
the other teams. The first player puts a large cork between his
teeth and says the words. He is not allowed to touch the cork
with his tongue. The other teams must try and understand
the question and answer it correctly. The player who speaks
the question may have to repeat it several times. The first
team to answer the question correctly wins that round. They
ask the next question. The members of each team take turns
to ask the questions.

Hot and Cold

Play this guessing game in a room at home. All your party guests can join in.

One player goes out of the room. The other players stay there and decide on an object for him to guess. He is then called back into the room. He has to try and find the object. As he moves about, the other players say 'Cold' when he is far away from the object, 'Warm' and 'Warmer' when he is getting nearer to it and 'Hot' when he is very close.

The guesser has three chances to say what the object is. It is a good idea to wait until he hears that he is hot because he has a better chance of making the right guess.

Everyone has a turn at guessing.

Cards in the Hat

You will need:
two packs of cards
a hat

Play this game in teams at a party. It is just as much fun with only two players.

Find two packs of cards with different-coloured backs. Each person has one pack. Stand a hat upside down on a flat surface. Now take it in turns to throw a playing card into the hat from about 2 metres away.

When you have thrown all the cards, count the ones that have landed in the hat. Each card from two to ten counts as one point. Jack, Queen, King and Ace count as two each.

If you play with two teams, the members of the team take turns to throw one card at a time.

You may be surprised to find how difficult it is to make the cards fly through the air.

Magic Egg

You will need:
an egg
a cloth

This trick could be part of a magic show for your friends.
They will be surprised to find that there is magic in an egg.

Ask a grown-up for an egg from the kitchen. Tell him that
you will bring it back in a few minutes without a cracked
shell!

The idea of the trick is to balance the egg on its end. This is
the way to do it. First lay a cloth over the table. Shake the egg
for a few seconds, then place it on its blunt end on the
tablecloth. As you put it down the yolk will settle and weight
the shell so that it stays upright.

Do As I Say

It is very easy to make silly mistakes in this game. Try not to or you will be out. Choose a leader. Everybody sits facing her. They must do whatever the leader tells them, and not copy her actions if they are different from what she says. For example, if she lifts up one arm and says 'Lift up one arm', you do the same. But if she jumps up and down and says 'Stand still', you must do as she says and stand still.

Anyone who makes a mistake is out. The last person in becomes the leader.

Coin Trick

You will need:
five coins of the same value
a hat

Here is some more magic for you to do. Learn the trick and then put on a show for the rest of your friends.

Tell your audience that you have put a magic mark on the coin that you are holding. They will not believe you, so you must try and convince them. This is how you do it.

You will need four coins like the magic coin with the invisible mark. Put them into a hat. Now pass the magic coin

around the audience. Ask everyone to inspect the coin very closely and to remember the date. When they have finished, put the coin in the hat with the others. Now close your eyes and tell your audience that you are going to pick out the magic coin.

It is very easy really. As the magic coin is handed around it becomes warm. All you have to do is feel around inside the hat until you find the coin which feels warm. Pull it out of the hat and show your audience that it is the correct one.

Unbreakable Balloon

You will need:
a balloon
sticky tape
two hat pins

Everyone will believe in your power as a magician when they see you do this trick. You are going to show your audience that you can stick a pin into a balloon without bursting it.

Prepare your magic balloon before you meet your audience. Blow it up, but not too tight, so that it gives a little when you touch it. Tie a knot in the end. Now cut two squares of clear sticky tape and stick them on to the balloon. Make sure there are no wrinkles.

Blow up another balloon, find a couple of hat pins and present yourself and your equipment to your audience.

Pick out a member of the audience and dare him to stick the hat pins into the balloon which has no tape. There will be a big bang!

Now tell everyone that you are a powerful magician and that you can prove it to them. Hold up the taped balloon and carefully stick a hat pin into each piece of tape. The pins should go through the rubber of the balloon underneath the tape.

Your audience will have their hands over their ears waiting for another big bang. There will not be one. What a clever magician you are! You may now take a bow!

Nut Hunt

You will need:
lots of nuts

There is something for everyone to eat at the end of this party game!

Ask a grown-up whether you can have some nuts, for example, peanuts in their shells. You will need a large quantity if you are having lots of children at your party.

Before the children arrive, go round hiding the peanuts. The garden is the best place but you could hide them indoors, asking permission first. Leave a number of peanuts in each spot so that the children do not take long to collect them all.

The person who finds the most peanuts is the winner. Everyone can then sit down quietly and eat their peanuts!

Red Rover All Over

The more players you have for this the better. Everyone lines up on one side in the garden or in a big playroom if you have one. Choose one person to stand alone, some distance away from the line.

When he shouts 'Red Rover all over', everyone must run over to the other side of the garden or room. The person who stands on his own tries to catch one of the others as they run past him. Whoever is caught stands with him as the children run back the other way. Together they try and catch more people. The game continues until there is one person left to be caught. He is the winner.

Card
Games

Beggar My Neighbour

You will need:
a pack of cards

You can play this card game with any number up to six. Deal
the cards as far as they will go.

The players do not look at the cards. They place them face
downwards in a pile on the table in front of them.

The player on the left of the dealer turns the top card of his
pile face upwards and puts it in the centre. All the other
players do the same. When someone turns up an Ace, King,
Queen or Jack, the next player has to pay him with some of
her cards. She pays four for an Ace, three for a King, two for a
Queen and one for a Jack.

If one of the cards that she pays with is an Ace, King,
Queen or Jack, the player on her left must pay her.

When a pay-off is completed, the last person to be paid
takes all the cards from the centre and puts them at the
bottom of his pile. The winner is the player who collects all
the cards in the pack.

Animals

You will need:
a pack of cards
paper
a pencil

Animals is best with five players. Before you begin, write the names of some animals on pieces of paper and mix them up in a hat. Each player draws one from the hat, and they then have the names of those animals.

Deal the playing cards as far as they will go. The players hold them face down in the palm of one hand. They do not look at them.

The player on the left of the dealer plays the top card from

her hand. She puts it face upwards on the table in front of
her. The player on her left does the same, and so on round the
table. Each player builds the played cards into a neat pile in
front of her or him. Only the top card of each pile should be
showing.

When two cards of the same rank (for example two fives)
come up on the table, the two players with those cards must
call out the name of the other player's animal three times. The
player who calls first wins both piles of cards. The other
players are not allowed to call. If one of them does call, he
must give up a card to the first two players.

When a player has no more cards to turn, he stays in the
game unless he loses his pile.

The winner is the player who collects all the cards.

Cheating

You will need:
one or more packs of cards

This game is a good one for parties because it can be played by any number of people. You can use up to four packs of cards.

Shuffle the packs together. If necessary remove a few cards so that everyone starts off with the same number of cards. Deal them out.

The player on the left of the dealer begins. She places a card face down in the centre of the table, saying the number of the card. For example she might say it is a five. The next player must call out six and place a card on top, continuing round the table up to King, then Ace then two, then three, and so on.

The trick of the game is that the player might not say the true number of the card that she is playing. So when a player has said a number, she can be accused of cheating by any of the other players. If she is found to be cheating she has to pick up all the cards on the table. But if she is wrongly accused, the accuser must take all the cards into his hand.

The game is started again by the player on the left of the accuser. He plays a card to the centre of the table and announces it.

The person who is the first to get rid of all his cards is the winner.

Go Fish

You will need:
a pack of cards

Five players is the right number for this game.

Deal five cards to each player. Place the rest of the pack face down in the centre of the table. This is called the 'stock'.

The player on the left of the dealer starts. She asks one of the other players to give her all the cards he has of a certain rank (number). To ask for the cards, she must have at least one of that rank herself. If the other player has some cards of

that rank he must hand them over. If not, he tells the asker to 'Go fish'. The asker must then take the top card of the stock.

A player can go on asking as long as she is getting cards from the others. If she has to 'go fish' and she picks up a card of the rank she wants, she has to show it before asking again. If she does not, the player on her left becomes the asker.

When a player collects all four cards of a rank, he shows them and places them face down on the table in front of him. These four cards are called a 'trick'. There are thirteen tricks in one pack. When all thirteen tricks have been put out, the game is over. The winner is the person with most tricks.

Old Maid

You will need:
a pack of cards

Nobody likes to be the Old Maid in this game, but it is still a very popular one. Any number can play.

Take one of the Queens out of the pack and deal out the rest of the cards as far as they will go.

Players look at their cards and take out any pairs of cards of the same rank (number). If a player has three cards of the same rank, he throws out two and keeps one.

The dealer offers her cards face down to the player on her left. This player draws a card out. If the card makes a pair with one of his, he puts them both aside with the other pairs. If not, he puts it in with the cards in his hand. Then he offers his hand to the player on his left who draws out a card. Play goes on clockwise around the table until one player is left holding one Queen. This is the Old Maid.

126

Slapjack

You will need:
a pack of cards

Any number of players up to eight can play this game. Deal the cards as far as they will go. Players put the cards in a pile face down in front of them. They do not look at them.

The player on the left of the dealer begins. He turns the top card of his pile face upwards and puts it in the centre of the table. The next player does the same, and so on round the table. Whenever a Jack is played, the player who first slaps his hand on it picks up all the cards in the centre and puts them on the bottom of his pile. The player who collects all the cards is the winner. If a player runs out of cards, she is allowed to stay in until the next Jack is turned up, just in case she can slap it before all the other players.

Pairs

You will need:
a pack of cards

You must concentrate very hard when you play this game. It is hard to remember where all the cards are.

The rules are quite simple. All you have to do is lay out a pack of cards face down on a large table. There should be plenty of space between all the cards and they can be at all different angles.

The aim is to make pairs with cards of the same rank (number). The player who collects the most pairs wins the game.

The player on the left of the dealer starts. She turns up any two cards. If they are a pair she picks them up, and puts them to one side, and then has another go. If they are not a pair she turns them face down again. The next player then has a turn. Each player's turn continues for as long as he turns up pairs of cards.

As the game goes on, and more cards are turned up, anyone with a good memory will be able to remember where the cards are. This will help him to make pairs. The winner is the person who has the most pairs of cards when all the pairs have been turned up.

Snip-Snap-Snorem

You will need:
a pack of cards

Here is another game for a crowd of players. Deal the cards
out as far as they will go.

The player on the left of the dealer plays a card to the table.
It can be any card she likes. The next player plays a card of
the same rank (number) if he has one, and says 'Snip'. If not,

he passes and the next player either plays a card or passes. Play goes on clockwise around the table. The player of the third card of the same rank says 'Snap' and the player of the fourth card says 'Snorem'.

The next round starts after the fourth card is played. If any player holds more than one card of the same rank in her hand, she must play them one after the other, and say the words to go with them. Each player must put out a card if he can. The winner is the first player to get rid of all his cards.

Games
for
Making Friends

Statues

Save up all your strength for playing Statues. It is a very energetic game. Play it with a group of three or more.

Choose one of the group to be statue maker. She spins each player around by the hands and lets him go suddenly. The player has to freeze into a statue when he stops. He is not allowed to move.

When all the players are statues, the statue maker has to try and make them all laugh or move. She is not allowed to touch them. The first person to laugh becomes the next statue maker.

Thief

You will need:
a blindfold (a scarf or a piece of cloth)
keys or a rattle

Thief is fun to play when you have a group of children who do not know each other very well. Everybody is in a circle. One person sits in the middle. He wears a blindfold. He also guards a bunch of keys or some other noisy object such as a tin of biscuits or a baby's rattle.

One of the other children is chosen as the thief. She sneaks up to the person in the middle and steals the keys. She then goes back to her place. All the children sit quietly with their hands behind their backs and look guilty. The person in the middle takes off the blindfold and tries to guess who is the thief (who must rattle the keys). He can then have three tries at guessing.

If he guesses correctly, the thief then goes into the middle. If not, the guard stays in the middle for another round.

In the River

Have lots of people for this game. Everybody stands in a circle. One person stands in the middle. When she calls out 'In the river' all the players have to jump forward. When she calls 'On the bank' they all jump backwards. This sounds simple but there is a trick. If the caller says 'On the river' or 'In the bank' everybody must stand still. Anyone who wobbles even the tiniest bit is out. The last person left is the winner.

Cat and Mouse

Play this outside or in a big room or hall. You will need plenty of space. You should have an even number of players – the more the merrier.

Players make a double circle so that there is one person standing behind another one, in pairs. One pair of players becomes the Cat and the Mouse. The spaces between the players are the mouse holes.

The Mouse can go inside the circle but the Cat is not allowed in. The Mouse darts in and out of the circle and the Cat chases him around the outside. The Mouse must not go in and out of the same hole. He must come out at least two holes away from where he went in.

The Mouse can stand in front of a pair of players. The back person of the pair becomes the Mouse and has to run off as quickly as possible. The first Mouse becomes the front person in the pair.

If the Cat is clever enough to catch the Mouse before two minutes are up, they change places. If not, choose a new Cat.

Sea Creatures

Have lots of children for this game. It is fun to play and fun to watch.

Everybody sits in a circle. Leave an entrance somewhere, several paces wide. Choose one person to be caller.

The caller goes round the circle giving each player one of these names: Cod, Lobster, Kipper, Crab. She then calls out one of the names. It could be 'Lobster'. All the Lobsters must jump up and run round the outside of the circle in a clockwise direction.

When the caller shouts 'The tide has turned', the Lobsters must turn and run the other way. When she calls 'The tide is in', they must go back and run through the entrance of the circle to their seats.

The last one back is out. The game continues, calling different names, and more than one name can be called at a time. When only one person is left in, he is the winner.

The Farmer in the Dell

All the children make a circle.

One person is the farmer. He stands in the middle of the circle. All the others join hands and walk round the farmer. This is what they sing:

The farmer's in the dell
The farmer's in the dell
Heigh-ho, heigh-ho
The farmer's in the dell.
The farmer wants a wife
The farmer wants a wife
Heigh-ho, heigh-ho
The farmer wants a wife.

The children stop moving round and the farmer chooses one person to be his wife. She goes into the middle with him, and the others move round them in a circle, singing:

The wife wants a child
The wife wants a child
Heigh-ho, heigh-ho,
The wife wants a child.

The wife chooses a child from the circle. The game continues
with the following verses of the song:

The child wants a nurse
The child wants a nurse
Heigh-ho, heigh-ho,
The child wants a nurse.

The nurse wants a dog
The nurse wants a dog
Heigh-ho, heigh-ho,
The nurse wants a dog.

We all pat the dog
We all pat the dog
Heigh-ho, heigh-ho,
We all pat the dog.

The game ends with everyone patting the dog. The dog
becomes the farmer in the next round of the game.

Killer

This game can be quite scary if you want it to be. It is a good one to play with lots of people at home or at a club meeting.

Everyone sits in a circle. One person goes out of the room for a few minutes. While she is away, the others choose a killer. He has to kill his victims by winking at them. The person outside the room comes back and tries to spot the killer winking by walking around the circle. She can have three guesses.

When a person is winked at by the killer, he has to fall dead into the middle of the circle.

When the killer has been discovered, he goes out of the room while the others pick a new killer.

Crazy Games

Wheelbarrow Race

This is a race for people to do in pairs. You will need a grassy area to play it on.

One person walks on his hands while his partner holds his legs up in the air. The aim of each 'wheelbarrow' pair is to get to the finish line as fast as possible.

They can swap places and have another race.

Wobbly Jelly

You will need:
a chair
two towels (or pinafores)
an old sheet or newspaper
a bowl of jelly
a spoon
two blindfolds (scarves or pieces of cloth)

This is a funny game to play if you are feeling in a very silly mood. You need two people to play. Ask for permission first.

Both put on your blindfolds, with the towels wrapped round you to protect your clothes. One person sits on a chair which is standing in the middle of an old sheet. The other person holds the bowl of jelly and feeds it to his partner with the spoon. Jelly everywhere!

If you have a lot of people you can make several pairs and turn the game into a race.

146

Nuts in Flour

You will need:
a bowl
flour
nuts
newspaper or an old sheet

You will have a very white nose when you have finished playing this game! Ask permission first.

Put some nuts on the top of some flour in a bowl. Take it in turns to try and pick out a nut from the bowl with your mouth. If you are playing this inside, put some sheets of newspaper down on the floor before you start. The winner is the one who picks out the most nuts.

Circus Elephants

You will need:
a pencil
paper

Find a big room or hall to play this in. Choose one person to be the circus ring-master. Divide players into two teams. They are the elephants.

The ring-master writes out twenty pieces of paper, each with the name of a circus animal or person – horses, trapeze artist, lions, juggler and so on. He places the papers here and there around the room or hall. He then sends the teams off to find all twenty papers. They have to try and remember the names on them, but leave the papers where they are for the other teams to find. After they have done this the teams go back to him and tell him the names they have remembered.

The difficult part of the game is that all the time the team members must hold on to each other and pretend that they are elephants. To be elephants, they each swing one arm like a trunk and take heavy lumbering steps. They must not lose hold of each other as they go round the room.

The winning team is the one with most correct answers.

Fancy Dress Race

You will need:
a lot of old clothes

Use a big play area for this crazy game.

Collect a heap of old clothes. Try and make up enough different outfits to go round all the players. You should have a hat, a shirt or jumper, a pair of trousers or a skirt and some shoes for each person. The funnier the clothes, the better.

Pile them all in the middle of your race track. Players line up at one end. When they are given the word 'Go!' they run to the pile of clothes and put on a hat, a shirt, a pair of trousers and some shoes.

They run in their funny clothes to the end of the track and then back to the middle. Then they take the clothes off and race back to the start. The first one back is the winner.

If there are a lot of you, you could play the game as a relay race.

Balloon Relay Race

You will need:
some balloons

Have lots of people for this game and play it outside. Divide everyone into teams and give each team a balloon.

The first person in each team puts the balloon between her knees and runs to the other end of the track and back. Using her knees, she then passes the balloon to the next person in the team. She must not drop the balloon. If she does, she must go back to the start.

The relay continues until all team members have run once. The first team to finish are the winners.

Harold and Gertrude

You will need:
an old newspaper
a blindfold (a scarf or piece of cloth)

Choose two people to be Harold and Gertrude. Blindfold Harold, give him a rolled-up newspaper, and put him in the middle of the circle of children. He calls out 'Gertrude'. Gertrude must answer 'Harold'. Harold tries to find her by the sound of her voice. He has to try and hit her with the newspaper. She runs round the outside of the circle.

When he succeeds he can take off the blindfold. Gertrude then wears the blindfold and tries to find Harold with the newspaper.

While this is going on, the other children will be in the way. They must keep out of the way of the newspaper, without letting go of each others' hands. Anyone who is hit by the newspaper is out.

Family
Games

What Animal Am I?

This is a simple mime game.

One person thinks of an animal and mimes its actions in front of the other players. They have to guess what the animal is.

Players take it in turns to be different animals. If the audience is unable to guess the animal, the player can help them by making animal noises.

Charades

This is a game for the whole family. It is a good one to play at a weekend, especially if you are staying inside.

The rules are very simple. Divide the players into two teams. One team goes out of the room to prepare their charade. They choose a word of two or three syllables such as 'cotton' or 'carpet'. They work out how they will act out the syllables and finally the whole word (*car,* then *pet,* then *carpet,* for example).

When they go back into the room they act the charade. Before they start acting, the leader of the team should show how many syllables the word has by holding up the right number of fingers. He should also show whether it is the first, second or third syllable which is going to be acted. If a syllable is very difficult to act, the team can act a different word which sounds like it, for example by acting *wet* instead of *pet.* The leader first holds his hand up to his ear to show that the word 'sounds like'.

The other team has to try and guess what the word is. When they have guessed, they have a turn.

Tell a Story

Here is a game that you can play in the evening before bed. Take turns to make up a story using some sounds instead of words while you are telling it. It makes a very unusual story.

Here is an example: Percival Porker was an (oink oink). One day he was feeling very (sniff sniff boo hoo). It was his birthday and everyone on the farm had forgotten. Nellie the (neigh neigh) always brought him a carrot to (crunch munch) but even she had forgotten this year. Mirabelle the (baa baa) usually came and (tra la la tra la la) 'Happy Birthday' but Percival had not seen her either.

Percival sat and (sob sob sob) all day. Then, at six o'clock exactly, there was a (knock knock) on the door of the (oink oink) sty. Percival pricked up his ears. 'Happy birthday to you' sang Daphne the (quack quack) with Nellie the (neigh neigh) and Mirabelle the (baa baa) and Reginald the (cockadoodle doo). Percival smiled and then he (ha ha ha) and then he (tra la la) for joy. The animals had remembered his birthday after all.